Write It Right

Writing an Essay

By Cecilia Minden and Kate Roth

Published in the United States of America by
Cherry Lake Publishing
Ann Arbor, Michigan
www.cherrylakepublishing.com

Reading Adviser: Marla Conn MS, Ed., Literacy specialist, Read-Ability, Inc.
Book Designer: Felicia Macheske
Character Illustrator: Carol Herring

Photo Credits: © Alexey Fedorenko/Shutterstock, 5; © Rob Marmion/Shutterstock, 13; © Bo1982/Shutterstock, 15; © Monkey Business Images/Shutterstock, 17

Graphics Throughout: © simple surface/Shutterstock.com; © Mix3r/Shutterstock.com; © Artefficient/Shutterstock.com; © lemony/ Shutterstock.com; © Svetolk/Shutterstock.com; © EV-DA/Shutterstock.com; © briddy/Shutterstock.com; © IreneArt/Shutterstock.com

Copyright © 2020 by Cherry Lake Publishing
All rights reserved. No part of this book may be reproduced or utilized in any
form or by any means without written permission from the publisher.

Library of Congress Cataloging-in-Publication Data

Names: Minden, Cecilia, author. | Roth, Kate, author. | Herring, Carol, illustrator.
Title: Writing an essay / by Cecilia Minden and Kate Roth ; illustrated by Carol Herring.
Description: Ann Arbor : Cherry Lake Publishing, [2019] | Series: Write it
 right | Audience: Grades: K to Grade 3. | Includes bibliographical
 references and index.
Identifiers: LCCN 2019006007| ISBN 9781534147195 (hardcover) | ISBN
 9781534150058 (pbk.) | ISBN 9781534151482 (hosted ebook) | ISBN
 9781534148628 (PDF)
Subjects: LCSH: Essay—Authorship—Problems, exercises, etc.—Juvenile
 literature.
Classification: LCC PE1471 .M56 2019 | DDC 808.4—dc23
LC record available at https://lccn.loc.gov/2019006007
Cherry Lake Publishing would like to acknowledge the work of The Partnership for 21st Century Skills.
Please visit *www.p21.org* for more information.

Printed in the United States of America
Corporate Graphics

Table of
CONTENTS

CHAPTER ONE

Sharing Your Opinion

"What do you think?" You've probably heard that question before. Someone asked for your thoughts or **opinion**. Maybe it was about a book or a movie. Sometimes an opinion is about an **issue**.

What do you and your friends talk about? Movies? Sports?

4

How can you share your ideas with others? You might give a speech or start a website. You can also write an **essay**. An essay has three parts:

- State your opinion or ideas in the **introduction**.
- Support your opinion or ideas in the **body**.
- Summarize your opinion or ideas in the **conclusion**.

Here's what you'll need to complete the activities in this book:

- Blank notebook paper
- Pencil with an eraser
- A computer (optional)

An essay is a piece of **nonfiction** writing.

CHAPTER TWO

What Do You Think?

Essays are always written in the first-person **perspective**. This means that your own thoughts and voice must come through to the reader. These are your ideas about an **event** or an issue.

For example, you could write an essay about the time you started a new school. You learned you could miss your old friends but still make new ones. An essay about an issue can explain your opinion about something. Maybe you think the local newspaper should have a section just for kids. Make a list of ideas and choose one for your essay.

Once you've selected your topic, think about your opinion of it. What are your thoughts about it?

Writing is done in one of three perspectives. Each one represents a different point of view. Essays are written in the first person. You will use the other perspectives for different writing projects.

- FIRST PERSON: the writer's thoughts. *I was scared going to a new school.*

- SECOND PERSON: the reader's thoughts. *You were scared going to a new school.*

- THIRD PERSON: another person's thoughts. *He thinks going to a new school is scary.*

ACTIVITY

Choose a Topic

In this activity, you will make a list of possible topics for your essay. Then you will write down notes on your idea.

INSTRUCTIONS:

1. Write down a list of possible topics for your essay.
2. Think about events or issues about which you have an opinion.
3. Choose one for the topic of your essay.
4. Write a sentence explaining your overall opinion of your chosen topic.
5. Make a list of at least three points to support your opinion.

TOPIC IDEAS

- Going to a new school can be scary. ✔
- The library needs more science-fiction books.
- The newspaper needs a kids' section.

OPINION AND THOUGHTS ABOUT YOUR TOPIC

My opinion is that going to a new school can be scary.

1. I started at a new school this year.
2. I was surprised to learn that I like my new school.
3. Now I am happy at my new school.

CHAPTER THREE

Write Your Introduction

Begin your essay with an introduction to get readers' attention. The introduction will contain several sentences. The first sentence might be a question or a fact. Let's say your essay is about going to a new school. It could begin with "Have you ever been the new kid at a school?" The introduction also includes the topic sentence. The topic sentence explains the main topic. For example, "I was nervous going to a new school, but now I really like my classes and new friends."

A new school can be an adventure!

Introduction and Topic Sentence

In this activity, you will write the first **paragraph** for your essay.

INSTRUCTIONS:

1. Write three possible first sentences to your essay.
2. Pick one that will make readers most interested in your essay.
3. Add at least two more sentences to your introductory paragraph. These sentences should state your opinion about the topic.

Sample Topic Sentence

IDEAS FOR FIRST SENTENCE:

1. I was really nervous about starting at a new school.
2. Walking into a new school can be a little scary. ✔
3. It is hard being the new kid at a school.

Sample Introduction

Walking into a new school can be a little scary. Everything is different. Everyone is different. There are so many things to learn and remember. I started a new school this year. But I've learned that scary can soon become spectacular!

CHAPTER FOUR

Write Your Ideas

The body of the essay comes after the introduction. It's where you explain why the ideas in your topic sentence are important to you. Refer to your notes. What ideas did you write to support the topic? Write a few sentences about each of those ideas. For example, you can write about the new school building, the classes, and the different activities. Help the reader see each of those things through your eyes. Use **adjectives** to make the writing more alive.

friendly

awesome

happy

big

yellow

Include details in your essay to make it interesting for readers.

You might prefer to type your essay on a computer.

The Body

In this activity, you will write the main paragraph of your essay.

INSTRUCTIONS:

1. Look at your notes on your topic.
2. Write a sentence for each of your ideas.
3. Put the sentences into a paragraph.
4. Use adjectives to make the paragraph come alive.
5. Write using the first-person perspective.

This year was my first year at Springfield Elementary. I missed my friends at my old school. I didn't think I would ever like this school as much as I did my last school. I didn't know anyone in my class. The building was different. I felt left out and a little lost. Then I met my teacher, Mr. Scott. He was so friendly and helped me to feel at home. He introduced me to two of the students, Tayler and Ella. He said they would help me get settled in my new school. They were awesome! They showed me around the school and told me how to find my locker, the gym, and the cafeteria. They told me about the clubs and how I could join. I knew I was going to like my new school.

You can make your essay serious or funny. Maybe both!

CHAPTER FIVE

Write Your Conclusion

End your essay with a summary of your ideas. Stating your main ideas again helps the reader remember what you wrote earlier. You might choose a **quotation** or fact that leaves the reader thinking about something.

Use a photograph or drawing to illustrate your essay.

Summary and Conclusion

In this activity, you will finish your essay.

INSTRUCTIONS:

1. Write the final paragraph of your essay.
2. Restate the main idea of your essay.
3. End with a quotation or fact that leaves the reader thinking.

Sample Conclusion

New schools can be scary. But finding nice people to help you makes everything go smoother. It really helped that my teacher and my new friends helped me find my way around. I will make a big effort to help other new students feel welcomed at my school.

Help the reader to remember your essay by crafting a strong conclusion.

CHAPTER SIX

Write a Title

Is your essay complete? Not quite! Read your essay again. Check for grammar or spelling errors. Once the essay is exactly right, give it a title. Think of a title that will make the reader curious. Instead of "My New School," your title could be "From Scary to Spectacular." Which one would get your attention?

ACTIVITY

Final Copy and Title

INSTRUCTIONS:

1. Type your essay or rewrite it in your neatest handwriting.
2. Give your essay a title.
3. You may want to include an illustration.

FROM SCARY TO SPECTACULAR

Walking into a new school can be a little scary. Everything is different. Everyone is different. There are so many things to learn and remember. I started a new school this year. But I've learned that scary can soon become spectacular!

This year was my first year at Springfield Elementary. I missed my friends at my old school. I didn't think I would ever like this school as much as I did my last school. I didn't know anyone in my class. The building was different. I felt left out and a little lost. Then I met my teacher, Mr. Scott. He was so friendly and helped me to feel at home. He introduced me to two of the students, Taylor and Ella. He said they would help me get settled in my new school. They were awesome! They showed me around the school and told me how to find my locker, the gym, and the cafeteria. They told me about the clubs and how I could join. I knew I was going to like my new school.

New schools can be scary. But finding nice people to help you makes everything go smoother. It really helped that my teacher and my new friends helped me find my way around. I will make a big effort to help other new students feel welcomed at my school.

Final Changes

Check everything one more time:

- Is my essay about my opinion of an event or issue?
- Does my essay have an introduction, a body, and a conclusion?
- Is my essay written in the first-person perspective?
- Does my essay begin with a sentence that gets readers' attention?
- Do I have a summary of my ideas in the conclusion?
- Does my essay have a good title?
- Do I use correct grammar and spelling?

Now you know how to write an essay! You may find that you want to write more essays. You have opinions on many topics. There are authors who are famous for their essays. Who knows? Maybe one day you will be one of them!

SCIENCE CLUB

Next, you could write an essay about going on a trip or learning a new skill.

GLOSSARY

adjectives (AD-jik-tivz) words used to describe nouns

body (BAH-dee) the main part of a piece of writing

conclusion (kuhn-KLOO-zhuhn) the end of a piece of writing

essay (ES-ay) a short written work about a particular topic

event (eh-VENT) something of importance that happens

introduction (in-truh-DUHK-shuhn) the beginning of a piece of writing

issue (ISH-oo) a topic for debate or discussion

nonfiction (nahn-FIK-shuhn) writing about real things, people, and events

opinion (uh-PIN-yuhn) personal feelings about a topic

paragraph (PAIR-uh-graf) a group of sentences about a certain idea or subject

perspective (pur-SPEK-tiv) a point of view

quotation (kwoh-TAY-shuhn) a sentence or short passage that is written or spoken by one person and repeated by another

BOOK

Minden, Cecilia, and Kate Roth. *Writing About Your Adventure.*
Ann Arbor, MI: Cherry Lake Publishing, 2019.

WEBSITES

Enchanted Learning—Essays to Write for Early Writers
www.enchantedlearning.com/essay
Check out some good suggestions for essay topics.

International Reading Association—Read Write Think
http://www.readwritethink.org/classroom-resources/printouts/
essay-a-30178.html
Use the Essay Map to help you create your essay.

INDEX

About the AUTHORS

Cecilia Minden is the former director of the Language and Literacy Program at Harvard Graduate School of Education. She earned her doctorate from the University of Virginia. Her research focused on early literacy skills. She is currently a literacy consultant and the author of over 100 books for children. Dr. Minden lives with her family in McKinney, Texas. She loves to spend time reading books and writing to family and friends.

Kate Roth has a doctorate from Harvard University in language and literacy and a master's degree from Columbia University Teachers College in curriculum and teaching. Her work focuses on writing instruction in the primary grades. She has taught kindergarten, first grade, and Reading Recovery. She has also instructed hundreds of teachers from around the world in early literacy practices. She lived with her husband and three children in China for many years, and now they live in Connecticut.